SELECTED POEMS

1955-1970

eldon grier

SELECTED POEMS

1955 - 1970

DELTA CANADA

ACKNOWLEDGEMENTS

Adam
The Canadian Broadcasting Corporation
The Canadian Forum
Delta
English Poetry in Quebec
The Fiddlehead
Fifteen Winds
How Do I Love Thee
Made in Canada
New
The Oxford Book of Modern Canadian Verse
The Penguin Book of Canadian Verse
Poetry of Our Times
Prism International
The Tamarack Review
The Unicorn Folio

*I'd like to thank the Canada Council for their help
in producing this book.*

Cover by Eldon Grier

$5.00 cloth, $2.50 paper

ISBN 0-919162-27-4

Delta Canada
5 Ingleside Ave., Montreal 215

TABLE OF CONTENTS

TO SYLVIA

MY COUSIN

My cousin was civilized,
he was born into peace,
there lay on his head
a dove's wing of hair.

With the greatest of dignity
he'd claim where he was;
I can always remember
the richness of those places.

For instance, the Alps,
in a gleaming sitzbath of car
my cousin in profile, a hat,
a caution that peace was in session,
                      he had been there
with peace attendant
like elephants to a lesser age.

QUEBEC

At steeplecock height
in a tousling wind,
bands of tourists,
ants in the spiral
dimension of birds,
stalk the pale
ghosts of history,
bet on each parroting guide
for signs of the dead.
But brother, nobody's home
except the river
with its carnival of ships
and the dizzying miles.
Forget your books and cameras,
dream you flew here
and that lunchtime never comes.
History is in the hotel lounges;
the delicate Wolfe
dying in a bed of flags,
or Montcalm, propped in the backstage
ruin of battle.

IN MEMORY OF GARCIA LORCA

García Lorca,
did you think
they'd let it go,
a flower in the lapel
of perpetual mourning?
Did you guess
the brilliant words
had made you alien
and (strangely)
evil?

Granada let you die
like any freak;
forgot the day,
forgot which pit it was.

Gypsies, farmers, generals,
priests, tourists,
and the quiet rich,
now pass blandly
overhead.

Oiga hombre!
Ask around.
Somewhere,
buried,
is a silver skull.

A "NORTH COUNTRY" ACCENT

I used to like
your north country accent.
You said "land" as if
you'd just baked it in the oven,
and "love" as if you had it
cupped in your hand.
There was always a glow of familiarity,
I swear your voice could reach out
and touch me on the arm.

A mystery deepened when you walked,
or stood contemptuously
at the stove,
            and it was pure sorcery
when you lay in the cleft of that old sofa.

I think you turned shyly away
from your own fierce whiteness,
from the shocking vigour of those three dark spots.

PORTRAIT OF A LADY

I know a lady
past middle age,
you may have seen her edging
round the corner at the bottom
of the hill.
She has a cataract.

I can fill you in;
she took her chance to be
brilliant as a toucan,
as cocky as her osprey plume,
as famous as her ostrich-feather fan.
She had insurance too;
a double-doubting profile,
a hideaway of books where she
could bill herself tragedienne
for every sweeping sadness.

You saw some indication
of the way things are
as she headed for the store,
in the smallness of her bones,
an air of resignation.

But however could you know,
as you watched her pick her
careful way along,
she rides a runaway.
Lurid as any ballad signed anon by the Master,
she goes galloping
perched atop the great brutish
nag of disaster.

DEBUT

Inside the joint in Lower Town
a black sargasso bobs and clacks,
the air is rank with sludge
of beer and cigarettes.
"Are you a painter (on my right)
I mean a painteress ?"
The question begs an answer.
Sirening with crescent white,
the shoulders of a singer coaxed
beneath the artificial sun.
A black haired one waves *quiet,*
at her side — becomes upset.
"Hey, cloudy man, forget the girls !"
This might be her debut.
Someone bangs a fist. The waiter scowls.
"Let's all go somewhere else !"
I made this note —
the shadows underneath her lids
were long and sable-soft.

TONY AT SEA

Tony has his work cut out
with his pretty new wife,
she seems to be always
threatening the blues.

The first time I saw him perform
was at dinner when
alert as a dog he set out
to reverse her natural bent.

It was great. Everyone
became involved; the young
waiter from Liverpool, the head steward,
his father-in-law ... Just the sight of him
seemed to make people uneasy.

He imitated me, and his old
college professor. He took off
rather too loudly for comfort
on a dozen types of Englishmen.

Like an old vaudevillian
he ate through an inventory of the
ship's food, and when she was past giggling,
produced a seedy birthday cake.

That did it. With a whoop not unlike a
bloodthirsty hound he burst triumphantly in upon
the still little stalactites
of her sadness.

HOW COULD YOU CAUSE SUCH WAITING

How could you cause such waiting
you're not that good,
dry hair, discoloured front tooth;
if it's lasting you're counting on, don't!

I'm a nasty fellow.
I'm due to foreclose some enormous debts.
All my life I've been waiting for someone like you
and I'll be waiting after you've left.

Even the weather's turned back
but you're a rainmaker aren't you, that's your trade,
flaming desserts your special,
throttling clocks into thunderheads.
By God you'd better be good
you'd better be great . . .

You coming to me me waiting, a farcical act,
bought you a ticket, found you a seat, all but
wiped the egg from your starving mouth.
It's Simenon you should be reading!

The conductor comes through, doddering father steam;
punch and smile, smile and punch.
Just what do you have to rate
such morbid attentions,
my priceless poet's shoulder?

GREAT TIMES

Those were great times
when my father would decide to take
us out on the town.
One night I remember we started with doubles
and by the time we reached the hotel
all tastes had become one.

We were still together
at the Russian place
        (the doorman wears an astrakhan).
"Where you bin ?" he asked.
"We bin dead," we said.

Then the fat headwaiter
advancing on us like a great
pimp of pleasure and
the tall bottles stacking up in the middle
of the table,
pulse became the beat of the band, and
the red walls, the red roaring in our heads;
        and how we smiled —
                great neon smiles
looping us around the table.

"These your boys, Chas ?"

How we smiled
                until the room
became the brown sea roaring, and mermaids laughed
below the seventh level of the sea.

FOR MERVIN

Before, all in black
you would have sat in the sun,
one of the privileged ones
debating
learning to affirm the old principles.

Tall in the manner of young Americans,
benign, ruddy-complexioned,
you now converge (you must)
on the habit of generations,
quit the job you so skilfully filled
to search back through time-landscapes,
through Rome,
bright and thin this autumn as
a newly cleaned masterpiece.

What you will find (your selection)
is so far undefined,
a new version of the David Star
softer perhaps around the edges
but still hieratic,
starfish-centred,
and spiked with cardinal points.

CLAUDE PICHER

Martyrdom not once but twice;
                  that is the plan.
The twin lobes of your brow gleam
with expectation. As I see it,
the winter is most likely to betray you;
most likely to smother the saints
                  in its fluffy pillow,
to blow their singing away
                  along its infinite grey ledges.

Turn from Europe, from the world,
and here's what's left :
seven kinds of sadness
                  panting out of the west,
and a pot-bellied stove for the sun.

SWIMMERS

Broad shouldered
patting their flat bellies
each shallow dive is a flourish of mastery.

THE SUN

Under the lids of the roof
the sun comes in discreetly
white, whiter than milk in a porcelain cup.

THE ILIAD

Old Greek !
Name compounded of semi-precious stones,
the sky of your epic is bluer
than fresco.
        Old fighter,
                axe-handler of fate,
and your Helen's ways as natural
as a yellow flower forever,
                sly meddler
slaughtering the black blood stalk
down to Astyanax.

THE BOMBING OF ALGECIRAS

Only one road leading into Algeciras —
no one thinks to disobey its finger.

Only one road leading into Algeciras —
and far from the broad-hipped generals.

Only one road leading into Algeciras —
and this begins to fill with life and importance.

Only one road leading into Algeciras —
and the sky is a neutral.

Only one road into Algeciras —
and dust promoting the way.

NORTHERN LIGHTS

It was astonishing, unique
and we bumped like fools in the dark,
danced and pointed like crazed astronomers.
The river, I cried, has rolled on its back
and these are its imaginings, the river has woken at two a.m.
and is writing the signs of its white forgetfulness;
the rock — I strained to say — the rock and the sea
can expose the ecstasy of its dream if it has to —
and we danced about in painful celebration.

OBJECTS IN A STILL LIFE BY MORANDI

These timid bachelors of space
cluster in a white-primed glow,
tapered, flaring, thick about the waist,
masquers of the young Tiepolo.

Cans and bottles tremble in a clime
the gentle artist activates with calm,
assemble on the beaches of the mind
where they finally belong.

MARINO MARINI

It is the portrait heads
that are sure to appeal to a writer;
old sharply expressive faces with the sun in their eyes
as the sun is in the open windows of my house today;
men wise enough to love their vices
with their virtues. Warmth and age favour flesh,
but bone is bone nevertheless.
The nudes are Pomona — the essential female fruit,
the ripe uncertain form surrounding a buried seed.
And last, or first, are the riders astride
their anthropological mounts, all sinew and outward thrust —
Marini the man, who has learned to grunt
and cry out his joy
in a radiant consciousness.

PICASSO IN SARASOTA

The room is raw and rare
with things seen for the first time;
women grown to flowers on
the dead weight of their mountain,
and a mask of horns tentatively
stitched with the new twine.
For the first time Love is a line,
and for the first time
loathing forms a spiny vegetable mass.
The sober side of dukes becomes
a monster stricken with the fury
of its annunciations and
the angels of the past generously pray
for what they cannot still.
Dürer comes upon the endless starfish
as he counts the grass,
and the lechers of Cézanne erupt
along the perfect smoothness of a hill.

SEASON OF UNEASINESS

Above the living and the dead —
a riverbed of stars, planets,
red and distant in relational
curves. I would like that special sound,
something so distinct that I might
sit in bars on one-time disaster
days and not be overcome by
the sadness of the exhausted,
or the early bluster of the
newest breed of world possessors.

The moon is up, a drifting cat's
paw covering its face — on blots
of grey the instant spoor of tracers
may have marked the day successful —
and as I represent the flux,
the play, the actual flow,
you may feel this moon, the atom,
Dogstar, Phoenix, everlasting stray
of light, the liquid consequence
of sudden memorial pain.

The element of stillness bears
the rattle of a train, dumb cry
of voices, helices of flies.
Exaggerate the poet's claim
for silences ! Place reticles
against the billion-terraced glass
of our inheritance ! I know
the rigid preachers' "peace" restrains
that greater truce when we survive
the relevance of our survival.

Across the lake the careful greens
are plastered with expended light.
The moon, grown shriller, bobs away
on islands of synthetic snow.
My care, my joy exonerates
the shadows from the crime of their
detachment — tomorrow though, the
twin cause of winner and loser
and paralysing words about
the full-faced warriors and saints.

FOUR PASTORAL STANZAS

1

With nothing but an average skill
the Flycatcher
makes his wonderful air-to-air strikes;
hollow bones a kind of weight deficiency
have made it possible.

... insisting on intensity of feeling,
insisting to the creature and the bone
where ecstasy and occupation
dissipate their lights
(with no Italian garden for the middle ground)
nothing but the city's lurid fire dome,
a broad processional of rimless days
for lighting up your arms ...

An average day of lunch
on Cheddar cheese and home-made bread,
tea, smoked meat, a buzzing in the head ...
a fist beside the steady lamp,
a breath outside to see
an owl flap whitely by the treed raccoon.

2

A climate of intensities
leaves the average poet hostile to
his neighbours in the wood; the anonymous
carpenter of windows,
the nameless fitter of the shingled roof.
A swim can break the mood
but not the sound which runs against the grain
and vegetates without the answering ear,
a growing threat behind
the textures of the spitted vine.
You at least, my love, are party
to this occupation of the "weight deficiency"
the other torturing innocence.

Music from familiar tapes,
a bored re-reading up against the screen.
The honey light brings on the cramp of night,
a miniature hysteria of moths . . .
fire shrinking in the ash.

3

Believing is the memory in art,
the clever surface bait which brings
the Sea-God to the level of the calm,
aberrant in tinder dry,
a bust of darkness as himself.

Perhaps he thinks the land
a tide of wrecks;
the web-like pressure of the pleasure boats
revives his fatal palms
and so he pinches the perspex of seas.
His famous sculpture shrinks the fishermen
to fly specks on the metal breast
and when he blurs they all but disappear
and as he disappears
he leaves the form of waves which
turn to words, and more than half
the wave is dark and mirroring
the mind of things ineffable in men.

4

Ineffable in one I should have said —
the Self in oceanic generalities.
In spite of this the poem finds its word
as darkly as the striking flesh
reveals its origins . . .

And so the way you look
is something in the way I work.
The huge return of light along the surface
of the lake has more of affirmation
than of stillness, more intention for the words
of mastery and love,
a passion from the frigidness of water mines
a final colour for the eyes' accustoming.

I walk, a man released from crime,
pick blackberries,
the partridge berries' poisonous red.
And now instead of mirroring and mime
the lake rots at my feet.

AN ECSTASY

1

Now the first condition is comfort;
and none of the gods could survive
this first condition.

Man must be prodigious, magical and just —

from now on

the poet will work in the bank
and the banker will write poetry,
to his own astonishment.

Craving fullness of life
we have fashioned
a clean blackness;
                inexplicable
                       expanding
out of the broken shape
of the past.

Closeness has become an infinity
purity has turned to spawning cells —

we are at the beginning.

Without regrets

look up at the colourless dark
that may soon become as familiar to us
as the green of grass.

Look about at our blue-bound world,
at the gentle rivers flowing like smoke,
at the women, young and erect,
at the marvellous invitation
of their breasts.
                Life must come from their life.
And beauty risk rebirth in strange surroundings.

2

In this city
where the flowers are prisoner
and the sea-porcupine a Gothic myth,

streets are widened, and immediately
the past flows out —
            a golden stagnant water.

Corners are straightened,
and old associations
lost forever.

There is a sadness in this . . .
we seem to be losing and losing
when in reality we are gaining.

We cannot as yet recognize the
expression of our happiness contained
in the clean new shapes.

But it is there and more.

Let us declare museums, and preserve
what was finest and most characteristic,

and let us build as we feel we must.

3

The long misery
                          with its stirring miracles
is coming to an end;

its answered prayers,

its prayers answered.

Festivity and penitence —
with a few elegant exceptions,
and the grizzly Horsemen
clattering out of the sky.

4

Go down to the market
and see the great red and white carcasses
hanging in the cold rooms.

(Meet the farmer and his family.

Their nationality is the country,
ours is the city.

It makes a difference.

Their complexions are different,
their manner is more open.)

You'll find eels and tobacco for sale,
and if you're lucky,
                        rows of flowers

out on the street;

        four-seasons, and roses,
                                small foster roses,
        geraniums and snapdragons,
                                greens,
        and mums; white, bronze and lavender, set
        against the umber richness of the vegetables.

        Imagine to yourself a festival,
        a day,
        with fresh cut flowers everywhere
        in the grey streets.

5

This lively morning

the young surveyors are warbling like Italians,
and the first wasp moves spastically over
ashen winter grasses.

The great vista of the freight-yard is an enigma
I leave to my children.

Conspicuous for their absence are gondolas
in the crooks of the old canal.

Loving praise, a schoolgirl reads aloud beside
the bubblegum machine.
"His strong arms were about her.
' You shall not go back into the chest tonight !' "
(A perfect age for a traditionalist, I think.)

The blackbirds have peacock feathers on their backs.

Bright red burns coarsely at the foot of
a grave.

A bald man, surely walking for his health, asks
eagerly, "How far before I get a view ?"

Bottle caps and shoelaces, things that have
survived the bottom of the white winter's well
receive my entire admiration.

Paradox, and the world unstitched for a new lacing.

6

This morning I looked for a poem, "Saltimbanques."

It had disappeared

as so many things are soon to disappear.

If you hurry
         to Europe
you may be in time to give a handout to the last beggar,
to see a king on his charger.
You may find nomadic street-performers in
some out-of-the-way place; the thin sad acrobats
of Picasso,
         and gypsies,
facing extinction like a tribe of aborigines, as
slack and incorrigible as ever.
You may feel there is nothing more moving than
fishermen pushing off from the sand in their curving boats,

and these will be the last to go.

But go they must, like old trees coming down,
like music from the streets.

And for a while
there will be greyness
and confused improvisation.

We shall feel outrage and despair at the sight
of our lives

until we recognize a new beauty
growing up about us, something less harrowing
and ornate — more serene,
lighting up the streets
              with clear slabs of colour.

But there is no need to explain.
It has its standards already,

you know what I'm talking about —

music, coming from the most unlikely places,
like new blood,

black and white, full of vitality.

7

Quebec was a fortress

and the black cannons still wait
on their tracks above the church spires,
commanding the approaches
to the close packed town within the walls.

At the top of Cape Diamond,

stretched out on the grass, I find a bigger
context for this hub of rock.
My daydreaming projects far beyond
the trajectory of any cannon.

It is all the same to me whether
I look up at the steep side or down.

Without a password I stroll about the streets

finding new answers to the plain arithmetic
of the windows, saluting the young women sweeping
in the doorways, invading the dormers
with unmilitary personages.

My rank is above rank.

I take the Governor's Garden for my own.

It was mine long before it was his.

I offer this poem in support of my claim.

I inform the newspapers
                    that it is not for sale.
It cannot be bought any more than one can buy
a garden in the sea.

The first clear day of a cold spring brings
six of us to Quebec

in high spirits.

The terrain is as sensational to us as it
was to the generals.

We find beauty shorn of doubtful motives.

8

By the twenty-sixth of May

the leaves are in small clusters,

the grass is emerald green beneath
the bell-cast eaves — in strips across
the saddle of the hill.

Figures in the niches of an old church
have been painted gold

against a hurrying overcast

the lime wash whites seem crisper than ever before
in their long history.

Three slender islands, I notice, are still awaiting
the explorers;
                    the vermilion of a spirited people.

Slippery, fresh cut logs are ochre and black,
and the apple trees,
                    astonishing orange flames.

They are straightening the sharpest corners
of the road.

The new cement plant covers farm land
down by the river's edge.
Its grey chimney brushes the sky
                    with two rosettes.
No one ever thought of so much industry.
Spring, and something more.

9

Prophecies are stated in grey and white.
Spells are stacked in the public libraries

without fanfare

forecasts arrive every instant,
                smaller than pepper seeds.

Gases burn with a wavering hiss
in the lovers' night

rock becomes light and sand becomes glass

and still we are cheated
of time and enchantment.

10

Have patience.

No matter how unsympathetic, how intractable
and fantastic things appear,

we shall eventually claim them for our own.

It has always been this way.

We shall envelop all structures and constructions,
all machines, and the whistling shapes of speed
in our customary joy.

We shall become accustomed to revelations.

We shall welcome surprise as no surprise —
as the sun comes up each day a quivering gold.

We shall invest function with the
fresh colours of our new materials.

Our plainness can only lead to fantasy.

11

More than most people,

the artist

is afraid of the gold gone from his eye
and the plum coloured tendrils grown
where once a god had sat transfixed.

He may feel something great and close to nothing,

a rare expanse of innocence.

To be lost is perhaps to stumble
                        on the Garden.
It has always been there
even before the first dramatic reporting.

How revealing it would be to find

carved into the trees

the signs and hearts of those who have known
its incomparable spell.

12

I can only sense what lies ahead;

the blue ceiling of Padua — but black,

glowing walls, a pure memory of southern flowers,

poems of the insatiable emptiness.

And for our comfort
and entertainment
resounding from undreamt-of distances,

the tiger-hissing, lion-roaring banter of actors.

13

Sensible is the label which most suits us —

especially the men

who lay great stock in honesty and good sense.

It never amounts to a passion
but you can see it on them,
                    a fine grey pencilling.

As a poet I need to experience ecstasy.

(English poetry never went crazy, a Frenchman said.
It was not a compliment.)

Our poets must give themselves to a kind
of unsensible madness;
they must hear music not meaning as they write.

Words must be clear bells,
or sound gravely along like horns.
They should detonate, explode like lightning
                            under the sea,
be silver wire, silk thread suspended,

sardonyx,

layers of white alternated with sard.

There are words that are the incomparable beasts
                        of our imagination.

Sound them.
Revel in the extravagance.

I wish to make literature, you say.

Oh, if only we could.

14

The greens are heavy,
                almost tropical this summer
because of all the rain.

I see the second country of the seasons;

in a housefly, bright as a bloodstone,

in the dead white face of a woman
                whose mouth
is a crushed carnation.

15

The river is blue

and gutters are generally grey.

Even here where the city squats
                    and performs its functions,

the odour of grease
is nowhere as strong as the summer's sweetness.

How would you like this city for your lover,
Apollinaire, sick ancient satyr,
                              could you succeed
where the bitter boys have failed,
dead poet of the rose decomposing,
singer of a sadness studded with chimney pots ?

Would you win

where the terrible smile of the mayors has spoiled,
where the profiteer grows odd and crooked
in his suffocating morning-coat . . .

the wedding having been indefinitely postponed ?

There is an exhibition of sculpture

where the bent-bow bridge shoots arrows
                              at the sky.

I know the city is deaf
                    and cannot hear
the insolent whistling of a new lover,

nor the queer footfall of an iron bird
which strides toward it
with the strength of a migration.

16

A famished man

I savour the smallest morsels;

a pale blue star at the bottom of a pond,

a rocking headlight swarming with locusts,

the sad mime of the juggler's curve,
an orange left to die on the empty stage,

whatever overflows the fences,

whatever escapes the prim snipping
                            of the gardeners
to bend in ripeness
over the granite snow.

17

The islands are black spears.

The summer green is all in blossom
                up the mountain slope,

I puzzle out

the blunt perspectives of the forest,
the shifting levels
             of the open wood.

The faithful one, the hunter, senses my return.

He sees me walk in circles

as a sign of repossession

I stop and name the trees : the shagbark hickory,
the linden tree, pine and cedar, silver maple.
I stoop to pick up sticks,
                and biscuit-coloured stones,
and stones that glint with mica chips.

I catch the smell of soaking earth,
            a metal in my throat.

I recognize the patterned zebra stripes of sumacs.

I fill and find at will.

A klaxon pheasant cry I cross with tauric blood.

I lie about and watch.

I crunch along the road to wake
the gold Mantegnas dozing in the rocks.

18

Sharon,
as you run ahead in this familiar wood,
I have no sudden intuition about the acorn's heart.
Did you know the conundrum of the oaks
was used as a magic by Druids?

I know this has no meaning for an eight year old.

Even so I feel its directions catching in your throat
like laughter, its solemn
nonsense spin my command
                    to the highest smallest branches.

You may try as I have done to lose yourself
in the orchards of the South.
                    It seems so desirable.

But there will always be a sympathy
as obscure in its origins as the quality of your colouring
which runs through the wood like a woven thread;
the sympathy which brings me back to these
gently sloping terraces.

What can I say?

For some there is the South, a sweet globe of fruit,
and for others, there is the dry
pointed riddle of the acorn.

19

Each year a new ring springs up around the city.

Look how fast we are growing,
chants the old chorus.

But it is not we who are growing,

It is the city,
dragging us along in the wake
of its transactions.

In this kind of growth we are less than a cipher.

It is time to unmask a tyrant,

I mean the clown who has us all by the hand
                              as if we were children.

We have come to speak nothing but its
crude slang of action.

Let us hear the sound of our own voices again.

Let us speak the dignified language of man.

Let us bring back from a bitter exile,
the colours of our exaltation.

20

I am almost asleep
with your poems on my chest,

Apollinaire

I am almost asleep,
but I feel a transfusion of fine little letters
dripping slantwise into my side.

MEETING

for John Glassco

God knows what another poet should look like.
When you came on with hands shaking
(after a taxi crash)
I saw nervousness and Englishness
and I
crossed arms against the body blow of meetings
after so much time alone.

Soon cognac froze
the sensitive word centres
so they came less jerkily
swelling up like a sleeper's heartbeat
then falling comatose.

"My book," I said, "my book,"
knowing you found me unlettered,
the ceiling pressing down on us like a silk cloud;
Beardsley, and Tennyson (neither of whom I had read)
then an Edwardian magician . . .

I finally came up with Clare
and a belch of optimism
which smelt, of all things, like clover.

MARIANNA YAMPOLSKY

You
haven't changed, Marianna,
buying glasses (tumblers) in a non-profit store.
I bet it's
a surprise for some chronic invalid
paralysed by the demands of his art.

I should have reminded you —
to draw
we once went up the mountains together,
the vultures would fly no higher.
You were
so quick on your feet, so businesslike,
I soon forgot my breathlessness and my battering heart,
and the drawings you did.
That day I saw
that a golden snakeskin was really the winter valleys below;
for you
the jagged erosions were moral, this was your faith.

Details are still so clear :
the evening wind,
the bus arriving late stuffed with whiteness,
and like a primitive panel, a face in every window.

I can remember
passing you twice on a stairway,
as usual you talked of thrift and arrangements
and mercifully never looked at my eyes.
How I
envied you then your intactness,
even your name which was you in a triptych of sound,
Yampolsky,
fruit, roundness, and finish —
what wouldn't I have given
then
for just *one* of those perfections.

GENOA

Genoa, city of the dream;
I have always known your evening hill cracked with shade,
and I have walked before the long turning face of your waterfront,
teasing the melancholy of voyages.
I have twice sailed off on a glassy calm blotched with smoke.
I have tried to forget the hired splendour of your stones,
and now I would be washed clean,
I would be free of these images,
of those generations, jealous and corrupt,
of the strain of supporting a continuous rain of dead merchants.
I am drunk in your bars,
stuffed in your confectionaries,
I have been sick in your gutters,
I have stumbled about with an aching bellyfull of rags,
I have curved into your heart on the sad black line of the railroad track
bringing nothing of importance.
I have sat in government arcades waiting to present my invoices.
At six o'clock I have watched the golden crater of the stadium emptying
                                        [its people;
I have gone home with them to boast of something now completely
                                        [forgotten.
It would take many poems, many crimes, to raze you completely :
it could start with the dynamiting of your famous cemeteries,
with the crumple of the clock tower of the Maritime Station into forty
                                        [feet of water
where it would cease to be, rippled and shadowless.
It could start with the pretentiousness of your songs flapping off in the
                                        [dead of night
with a tidal wave of lemon juice.
It could start with a hail of spectrum acids melting the roof tops;
white, blue, bronze and green.

I AM ONE WHO SLEEPS IN THE LAP OF AN OLD PORT

I am one who sleeps in the lap of an old port,
awakens to the sad cat cleaning of the waves,
shores up head with arm in the manner of Walt Whitman,
scrapes nail on toe to feel if it is really now.

Too familiar is the deaf-sight of the place;
peninsulas menacing like pineapples on a smooth plate —
tonsils in a blackened throat, musical pudenda
to the oldest of the raving life surrogates.

Growing slightly sick of my extended day
I slant a string of words at prominent solemnities,
stretch to see them stop racked zig-zag in the picture light,
grow sharper and more lyrical than was intended.

Dreams can bring about a synthesis of time;
telescope to plausibility the passion of a dozen lives,
take and then deracinate the boy who seeks
hypnotic landscape rather than a fusion of the first felt.

I am one who sleeps in the lap of an old port
nourished by the claimless blizzards of its visitations,
half alive to forests of retorts and spines
and caissons rusting down the dangerous water drops.

LA MAISON NATALE DE PICASSO

The place where Pablo Picasso was born is number thirty-six
on the third floor in the Square of Mercy (power, discretion);
a model of the age, five neat tiers of oven doors
on white plaster, sand-domes stencilled in the sun's quicklime.

In the afternoon of its usefulness it stares out without
benefit of trees (a note on the painter said that these
were fortunate times, although 'the incident' happened here).
Having no glass, the windows reflect a blaze of interior coolness.

From the firm white shaddocks of his mother's breast
the artist here received his first instruction, and if her dress
closed all to the neck — the slightly ovaled eyes the firm catholicity . . .
'If someone were to tell me you had sung the Mass . . .'

Hardly unfortunate to be born in Malaga (in a town whose top
looked off to where sea lay negligently, weighed blue across
the palisade of palms) sister oval-eyed, father like a stick of shade,
waves of fashion coming down the line from Barcelona.

KISSING NATALIA

Invention begs from door to door in the indescribable darkness,
a chorus of animals like canned laughter. I had it planned,
drunk though I was, to drive you to the edge of the town
and when you said 'thank you' as you always did, I was going to kiss
[you.

This was the plan and in the calm of decision I got you in,
passed houses drawn up like fanatical serfs, my thin excuse
trailing lifelessly after us like a rodent tail. (The general's
coming, boys, and his aide-de-camp and faceless mariachis from the
['gatos'.)

The engine slowed as my heart rose, your profile, dumb in the light,
came to the edge of town, looked off to stepping stones
which glowed in the shadows, to total darkness, and Lord knows
[where.
You said, "thank you," and so I put my hand there and kissed you.

Were you scared ? It must have come like a moon pie in the face,
and unprepared for an instant, the trembling ring of your lips
held me as a lover. The place reeked of the chemistry of rivers
I remember now, and your mouth left the slightest aftertaste of earth.

ON NEHRU AND A DEAD MEXICAN

Nehru is seventy but his walk is young, and the girl
who hands him a single flower does so unaffectedly. Beauty,
certain values that is to say, enclose him protectively;
leggings, rosebud, cap; peace and gentleness for an old man.

A ban on slaughter ! The walls of *this* town are haunted
by the sound of animals dying. *(They* would have skulked
or come at that first flying-machine with flashing machetes ...
the Indians brought it hay and I don't call that an act of naivete).

To whom should we appeal — the Revolution — men may feel
anger, or toll the bells for forty days and it would make
nothing but a shuddering silence. Beauty is the total stranger;
total and complete each time the lamb bleats through its terrible wound,
the horse confused, and then lustily skewered in the gut.

A friend said *he* had been lying there for two days in plain
sight.   There was no trick in throwing down a few flowers,
but to drag *him* to the shade, to budge *him,* that would have been
[suicide.

MOUNTAIN TOWN — MEXICO

Arms at my side like some inadequate sign,
I lie awake in a dark room in an alien country.
While plates of frost slide past my face, and needles
cluster in the crêpe-like air, my friend who has made
his adjustment, urinates into a bucket with a thunderous ring.

I must impress myself with certain things;
the honesty of mountain people, the lightheartedness
of a people never conquered by arms — and yet
the monster of the mines lies dead beneath their homes,
its scattered mouths decaying in a final spittle of stones.

Into this piled-up town beneath astringent stars
what did we bring with us that is simple and hopeful —
into this confusion of times ? Breadcrumbs for the blister
of the floor, bottles crowding off the ebbing surfaces,
memories of love, perhaps the gentle trauma of our intrusion.

A jukebox rumbles out a tune, the singer
holds her sex against my abstract form. We are the angels
of ironic movement, she and I. Our pleasures
are more permanent than the mountains here whose marrows
fired in a day form quickly into sediments of tragic angularity.

I lie awake until the blackness burns to filaments
of tired red. A horse sparks up the cobblestones.
A voice speaks cleanly from the stage of cold beyond.
No spout of sunlight ever entered to my bed, but stealthily
an orange cat comes snaking through the door in search of food.

VIEW FROM A WINDOW — MEXICO

The tenderness so hard to swallow
is partly the two flies settled in her hair.
Her mouth opens to the soothing air,
drool scabs curving down from its edges.

And her brother whom she holds shyly for me to admire . . .
the mess of mucous and the clinging feeding flies . . .
awake, a toxic film covers his eyes
shifting mechanically in patterns of escape.

Across the steeply climbing flat-faced street
at the six vertical ochre strips
her older sisters, short skirts flaring from the hips,
emerge and blow away buoyant as wasps.

Beauty complicates the average squalor,
carries the unpredictable like fallout
into the brutal levels, burns about
the ruin and the green vine with its yearning.

She hangs around; she says she's eight.
Her name is tuned for ceremonial complaint;
mine is, that dozy flies can travel here without restraint
in the gentlest of hatchures.

EMPALME ESCOBEDO

A yellow chair,
the clock — a lyrical moon,
the window-square
and the slumbering bars
of the sky,
a dog infested with fleas.
A view from the lover's eye;

a view of strawberry dress,
brown and black
and dusky, mottled
with green —
the virgin girl who
holds at her breast
a lamp of ice-cream.

A view of the dead in
a flickering wood;
a child with
a crown on its head,
the miniature bones at its eyes
which give the effect
of noble disguise.

A ceramic of streets,
the cannoning blurt
of a train,
the farmer who stops in the
night of his hat,
the white of a wrinkled shirt,
a lumbering cat.

VAN GOGH AT ARLES

Because he groped his way down to the Mediterranean
having first picked through the clinkers of compassion,
risen and closed the door on some mindless whore
he had designated as love's bride . . .

and then the friend comes on from Paris, smooth and opinionated
spouting latin arrogance and the good life,
and poor Van Gogh unlovely in the carroty sun
thrown back hard into London
and the grey Brabants of his misconceiving.

An artless grandeur
as he stands manacled to his palette, a quaint cosmogony
of friends turning about the corner house slower and slower —
zodiacal signs, luminous clods of provincial lust,
or like the postman Roulin
almost rabid with mediocrity.

Pervert in the still arena of Arles, trussed to his awkward gear
pushing the last Dear Theo into the box,
the suns pursue him up the avenue,
the butcher's paper with a severed ear.

OF WALLS AND THE SEA...

To end these familiar epics
               we must all agree
to mothball the fortressed cell,
to stitch the hero, still brandishing an oar,
on strips of formally tempestuous green.

Unusual methods are usual.
                    In another day
Carpaccio slew the Dragon
          with some beautiful notes on the weather;
and the Master of Aix ...

but this is more in the nature of plastic prophecy.

                  Probably
the classic example of method
was when several merchant princes
            acting together as a republic
married the sea,
            and the Republic consisted of
lights, vistas, pagents, architecture, splendours,
and some painfully secular boats.

The marriage lasted,

and agreeable persons are likely to say
that the sea was the luckiest.

ON AMBIGUITY...

Ambiguities,
sovereign states of complicity,
whatever persists in provoking the Great Mystery,
                              surely
we must tangle with the living live,
     with the stubborn bedrock of matter,

and we must die with conviction of regret.

Summer is busy joining us into its mists.
Already the sun possesses sparkling reaches of the lake,
its presence is like celestial bees
swarming up through the treetops.

I see Monet, dew on his beard, sweat on his girlish face.
I proclaim that he is the greatest of seers,
     a spirit whose dream was the flesh —
and here is Sisley, gentle, inclining to his heavy Hera-wife.

Some urgency towers me into the skies.
                              This is the only discovery!

These are the lands!

Summer has placed six suns on the brace of my steering wheel.

Poems, I know by now, go out like stars.

ANSWERING MAIL NEAR GENOA

My mind revels in this saturated bitterness,
acid sunlight
on the stony strands,
                          instant and intolerable froth,
enormous birthmarks on the sea.

"Pleasure hearing your poems," the letter goes,
                                  "... nostalgic
                                       [moments.
                      We think
one of the compensations of middle age is less drama."

Desperate birds below the car, a bridge, another town ...
Columbus sailed away from here. Columbus drowned himself
in distances. Beckman walked a yard
to pull the curtain cord !

                    "You must
take us as we are ..."

The surf explodes, the human crust in every cove, the cupping
of the wind against the cliffs ...
Montale lays his spell along the chalk. On lonely walks
he drifts through veils of his ambivalence.

I live, dear R. & P., I live in this horizon line —
it has no roses, vines, fishermen, commercial status ... and no age.

ON THE SUBJECT OF WAVES...

Mountain teeth, tips of anemious rippled stone,
a glacier of white cloud settled into the tilting passages :

Are you there, Li ?

Are you there in the mists, Li Po ?

If I ring your two-change name against the massive greys will you
[answer ?
On this day and in this location can you see how it is with us humans ?

There are greens about me here, and the pressure of the soft gloom,
animals in the rising fields.
                              Men I shall never see
stand in the doorways of their huts like true sentinels of life.
There are chimneys behind me rolling up the first balls of pale smoke.
A high plateau above, ceaselessly swept with tears of anemia,
before me, and always in my mind is the shape of peninsulas
as insistent as a black mirror.

The empty truck, traumatically still;
a score of men loosely grouped beneath a tree.
                    The stillness is the echo of an explosion !

I find the burlap square in the centre of the road
and I know that beneath it there is a dead child.

Is this what you meant by "waves," Li Po ?

ON CITIES...

If not conquerors
then why not a culture hero ?
Nezualcoyotl, Pachacuti (who was both),
sacred urbanists from the green apices of the continents
from the white lipped cordillera of Peru.
                    Of Tenochtitlan
Bernal Diaz de Castillo says, " 'Like a dream ... the enchantment
                    they tell us of in legend.' "
                    (This sort of talk from Cortez' men !)
Again,
        Cortez : "More beautiful even than Seville !"
                                        And yet
how completely they destroyed it all
as if the world could tolerate nothing but the European imagination;
and so in Europe's way the cities grew on other cities —
blue and grey, brick and sullen spots
                        in the
pitiless sunlight of America.
About our present day pragmatic landscapes
certainly
        more than we can tell...
men change slowly (unenthusiastically)
but caught so closely in this greatest swell and stray of city growth
                    much has broken loose :

mercantile is loose in tropic, creature-love in spirit lamp,
sky facades —
            bioptic magic.

... the purest stele or a shell of some impersonal kind of strata ?

PORTRAIT OF LIPCHITZ AND HIS WIFE BY MODIGLIANI

It shows
the pain of Dialogue
the man as cockerel of rain,
the hatchet man of tedious associations;

as tan
as witty wife is white,
as spurred as she is oval-poised
and redolent of love ...

The world would crack apart
if this should last
in even
one particular face.

Correct me
if the image of a crab,
a cup of metal on an iron tree
is not the way
this magic
passes
to ambition.

PICASSO AT ANTIBES

He came to Antibes ready for the competition;
a thousand platters dropping from his cloak, his eyes
perpetually awake like a pair of perching owls.
There wasn't a day when back to the sun
he couldn't upstage his own production, or drag
the golden loaves of his fingers from the irresistible light.

Poets came and shedding their decorations
wrote voluminously about his face of bread; a team
of photographers chosen for their faith
diced their luck against the smarting walls, blacked
the diamond peepholes of the castle at the stroke
of noon, cooed the phrases of their shaven dean.

It was women though who roused the vice of
his creation with their look of coins; trite and wise
they laced the rhythm of his days with gifts of food
and paregoric drops. Only claims of innocence,
he knew, could guarantee this staid support and such abuse
of love. His flowered brush was wet.

The master's T-shirt hung about the town like
an emblem of the Seasons. A foil for the
unscored zinc of the sea, the old man's tom-cat head
rose above the peeling rails beside the rocks
like a proclamation of magic. Even where the queasy sails
hung languidly, one felt his sharp emprise, the barking of his clock.

PICASSO EXHIBITION

I might have guessed that the school girls would accept his hegemony, and I noticed at once a peculiar relaxation emanating from the cloakrooms.

It was a Saturday to remember : guards guarding the treasure, families plastered on the extra chairs, mothers describing parabolas to their friends, fathers bottling offences.

SUNDAY — MEXICO CITY

In the burning eye of the fruit fly
the phoenix dies a ritual death of nursery rhymes and laughter;
windows lose their sight dreaming of jasper and plumbago;
twisting segmented tails, the movie queues have infested the roots of a
[skyscraper;
the sun has burst its blood on the Edificio Colon;
without gas or electricity the people have dispersed, leaving the inland
[sea of paving to its fast, its steady polaroid thirst;
creosote dries to an ash on the empty X of San Juan Teotihuacan;
a great research has been lost in an acre of broken glass behind the
[cathedral;
the plan that's brought to light in the golden tooth of the waitress
has haunted the couple who rise and fall in the park like the history
[of nations.

DAIANEIRA

She must have enjoyed
the Centaur's fatal attentions
(her husband was a freak;
she'd found this out avoiding a monster).
Her girlish distractions
like her ordinary wishes
drew down poisons
from the air.

BIRTH OF VENUS

(after Botticelli)

A God success
to shock the Gods;
starting as it did with castration
and other disturbing events.
Following the froth
some lyrical touches; rapture
of the Shell, the Winds
as youthful lovers
charged with her initiation.

MINOTAUROMACHY

Laddered for escape
    the poet turns to wonder and perceive,
  Christbeard, naked for science,
        loinclothed for God.

    The central character, the monster,
landed from his bark is scooping the
shadows for victims,
    flushes medihorse
      and beautiful ghostcarnage.

Innocence, of course, he toucheth not,
  nor breaketh he the lamp so loath to light;
flowers poetical in fright
say bye to the mummy death.

    Women, special case, are quite
preoccupied with doves;
    Madonna of the testicles and
         Beatrice ofthespeechlessgrace.

The mythic sea is plate
    the human puzzle ready for the heap.

I WAS BROUGHT UP BY THE SEA

1

I was brought up by the sea
I felt I'd never lose its weedy taste its garden in my hair
I used to examine it with primitive instruments
proving truth or so I thought

I'd touch its poisoned cold
but my counterspell was more than adequate
sea in which rails are engulfed
in which iron breaks an egotistical silence

I once saw something drowned
and it had lost its name
white with exceptional legs it was growing out of the rocks
I knew nothing of tragedy

confront me and I always broke I'd become habituated
if I claimed a city it grew bulbs across the roofs
it chopped the streets I chose like a chromium guillotine
head from body body from head
I was innocent and rich.   I even felt as if
the sea were looking for me ...

2

what should we domesticate
what should we contaminate with our ideology
the sea with paws withdrawn cats paw sphinx paw
the wonderful arm machine of water
I ask you
has the alphabet died
is there a single word which doesn't respond
like servants torn from sleep . . .

I lived in the soil of my senses glowing and disassembled
the fisherman's boat the chambered-heart indenting was my music
the fog was my night
my punctuation ships as thin as wafers

open mouth and royal ears I came to the sea
in its packing case of stones
its grainless cut across the day
I played the North like an empty card
I read the sun like a broken seismograph

3

through stillness what have we presumed
why have we not created from our emptiness
here was the sea's effluvium sharp and explicit
the rhythmic threshing of stones
was itself an ageless application ...

through my personal bead of glass I played examiner
recording the passing of things
voiceprints on the oyster of the sky ...

from the linear shadow explorer's brass
from the cliff of my uncle's house from its shin its ankle
its crusted toes
from the fly-blue wedge of the land
the hunter hunted the sulphurous detente ...

I was brought up by the sea
its vast anatomy of weight
a list erasing names
rictus holy gape

NEW YORK SPRING 1966

a certain day in spring
supermasters swooping about me in their playful capes
I emerge from a violet atavism weighing some tidy risk
my companion has a bellyache he says
should I be thinking of food

a certain day to be precise
the vast corruption of hotels like ruined constitutions
starving hallways doors adrift in varnish
a suffocated window
should I breathe this oxygen of light

this spring a vast hotel
pillows pigeons peopling the air
rainwords slicing corridors swelling status quo

adolescents plotting into shirts
plodding with their frozen duchesses

DON'T FRET

don't fret
I'm tethered to this chair
you see these eyes this arc
that's where I am
knocking on faces like a mediaeval beggar

noses are worn in profile
that's my foreign news
and the news from home —
I'm on the point of announcing
the GENIUS OF WAXWORKS

confidentially though eyes examining saints
or auto-issuing instant and final doctorates
or juicing a patch of skin
like a drowning man
remembering his women . . .

I'm here I'm in your presence
waiting for Godot or father Death
or for some final theme whose absence
only now disgraces me

A PLACE SO DECENTLY LIT

riding the
top of the road
brutal flaying
but for
        PROTECTION
this world we've made
suburbs
blooming exhaustion
terrible trick of fate
                a place so decently lit
feel sensitive tonight feel sick
I howl for the future like a dog
emptiness and fuck
miracles and slack
        a place
        so decently lit
        so nothing
        &
        so perilous

A SHOPPING LIST FOR ENGLISH CANADIANS

Let us stir in the surface of the landlocked lake of yesterday's dessert.

Let us compromise the life appointment of the magistrates of the
[vigilant tower.

Let us poison the moonlit style of the pimp of the turreted garages.

Let us hurdle the lust of the landladies of the self-made virtuosi.

Let us capture the wings of the tasseled bit of the charge of the
[cereal cowboy.

Let us master the contours of the cattle skulls of the metropolitan police.

Let us crush the persistance of the paperweight of the highly
[mortgaged factories.

Let us wrestle the morbid vagrancy of luck through the guillotine of
[the neighbouring doorways.

Let us trap the sacred deterrent in its intricate breast-work of
[office furniture.

Let us break to the crawl of the tremulous lights on the banks of the
[chasm.

Let us howl to the hollow flame of the windows of the beach cottages.

Let us close with the wrack of the fumbled wife in the razored arms of
[the shutters.

THE WOMEN OF QUEBEC

Once they lay breeding as the sky pried open the shell of winter.

Once they lay breeding the arms of the evergreens pinioned with snow.

Once they lay breeding the threat of death like a coffee stain.

Once they lay breeding nostalgia stamping in the threshold.

Once they lay breeding the bellwinch summoning the forest.

Once they lay breeding the martyr's wit.

Once they lay breeding the sour dawns the flour of misery rising in
[the cradles.

Once they lay breeding the tribal scar their bodies of rush in America's
[vein.

Once they lay breeding the pungent smell of slavery in their hair.

Once they lay breeding the crackle of billboard pistols and gum.

Once they lay breeding the terrible chansons of their fate.

Once they lay breeding collections of grist and plastic revolution.

Once they lay breeding a film in which everyone was a negress.

Once they lay breeding the eye of the ptarmigan the plumasier's tunic.

EUROPE IS DEAD

Let me walk with you (violently)
bump you, breathe my way back into reality.
Europe is dead; its great ideals
can be washed away like the paint spots on your skirt.

So that old placenta bursts
(I'll be gone by the birth) and the
anguished rush of heroes, saints, perfectionists, form-makers . . . ugh !

Let me sweat and knead your hand,
let me strain to possess the lengths of my crooked legs.

GIACOMETTI

there was the final day of his double identity
the last of his kindly animal entrances

the longer he lived
the more his sculptures resembled him
the longer he lived
the more his stove became angelic

ah those piles of brushes
little prison sentences
and the widowed chair

his intention
was like a table
without graffitti
or mythic hair
like the ragged lightning
in bottles

MORRICE

1

Ideally you should be
easy with drinks
and I easing the
torture of my affections . . .

The Cycle (unnamed)
the rigorous silence
surrounding our work
is patent defence
of the exotic,
the price of our
one-eyed birth.

O listen
Time leaves Time
like an accident
to a train of barges.
You (in a secret
shade of brown)
lurk in the lining of
your pictures, sapping
the lights, thinning
the words of this poem.

But an accident
cannot postpone illumination.
Light is a friend, sweet cockroach,
your secret is shared.
The crescent miniatures
may yet be laid in the vault;
the diaries of disuse
will find their way
to the administrator's table.

2

Experts in fade-outs and
amputations, we've shared
experiences; balloonists cutting
the thin dry skein, we
drifted on Europe's centre.
We dated nothing, why should we?
Our shadows fell between
the blueness of origin
and the darkblack stain of
our exhausted senses. Exile? No.
Exile is what one man
does to another.

... from the same city,
the same streets.
at Cushing's Island
(ten years after your death)
the ward of venerable women,
one bald, and one with
a frosted eye — Ste. Petronille,
St. Malo under the pebble —
clouds of northern France,
the mouth of the Rance
crowding with humps —

The warmth you felt, the
cramps you had in shadowed
streets are no longer
one man's business; the gentle fits
that laid you in the sea
like a diuretic.
Who locked us from the house
did you know? It was
the nurse with her
shameless hands wasn't it?
Who drew the blinds and showed us
the grandmother of colours?
Who touched the fruit of
the cellar? A judgement was made
a division (I sense
you agree) and style was born
as if by accident.

3

Photograph

To acknowledge your
presence, I know, would put you
beyond the veil of isolation,
it would confirm your
stroke of nerves so
hard to conceal, your lifelong
honeycomb of debility.
Where is luck in this face ?
Where is Monday ? Where
confession our daily bread ?
O face (unwrapped as mine
is to be) unclaimed when
the period fell
in blossoming and fire.

Wastefully I mourn
the park, sick, I stretch a
final tenancy though
yours could take its place;
your steady emanations
your half-light, private,
shining like morocco.

4

A period ends. As
I said, Time has met with
an accident (your Time)
a cleaving from the future,
a cesura.
A scholar I search
for your spoor of ash in
the suburbs trampled into life.
A Schliemann I trace
your fading apparatus,
the wire chair, the awning,
the finger smudge at
the edge of the myriorama.

O to have sorted your mail,
to have caught you
at your exercises,
to have heard your paintbox shut
(evening's tiniest punctuation) to
have found your opinions of
Maugham, of Bennett
of Condor, of Henri Matisse
drawn up like a will . . .
this to you O master,
and this O fool . . .

but that would be anomaly,
unreal, a miracle, betrayal,
a successful operation.

I send you greetings
from your mute cousin, Garneau,
your cousin washed up on the shore,
your cousin scratching dirt,
your cousin lying blue
by the tailpipe.

IT WOULD BE A JOKE

it would be a joke
if I managed to live beyond
some terrible physical upheaval
the floors gone
the stars invisible until further notice
the helmets of beauty parlors pushing out of the mud
                                    like Easter eggs

MY WINTER PAST

I owe nothing to winter
because it is not my way to be cold
or to be covered like furniture in a deserted house :
my father was flickering warmth;
feelings poached in the living white of my mother's passionate isolation;
my brother's hands said what he had to say (and died without saying).
I wore down the evenings with mirrors of flesh and wool.
I trampled a landscape of frozen hysteria,
cried out fear with my winter joy.
A child with needle in brain,
I armed myself with the physical sweat of kitchens and drugstores
and gravies and lightbulbs and dreams ...

What was queer
was an all-deceptive peace :
midnights of burgeoning snow, charcoal cupboards of heat,
the actor's clap of the door — a knock on wood,
a single breaking wave in the family of stillnesses;
smoke behind the trees so pure so very far, tumescent, imperially weak.
                    ... Beneath a continental grey
                    inside the brilliant tear of cold
                    in the visceral voices of women
                    in the fossil of the windows
                    in the ragged nostalgia of sugar, of fever
                    in the fruity dampness of wool
                    in the licorice veins of my sensuality.

#4

Puppet girl pimple-starred
enters from the aisle her
walk a demonstration of
walking her feet as fine
as almonds pared from
loveless pod of our technic
God is Love and/or Necessity
(Shelley's Word) Enlightenment
(untried) is oriental dogma
still unravished bride of
Zen   Couldn't cross her legs
She's beautiful if life is
that if wood if walk if
holy plastic hinged Puppet
pressed in door impresses form
which Godness never was

#5

Holy Family with Ste. Anne
arranges itself in the
general modernity (sic) Anne
inclines towards the Babe
(perfume for the sweetness
of sentiment   outward signs
of adoration) Joseph cor-
poreally absent features none-
the-less What curbs for changing
world What bare familiarity
(that is) what perfumed womb
the Promise   Meantime city
smells of cat River hints
at abnormalities Light suspects
the badlands the ba Christlet
turns (a lexicon rephrased)
to strike with wooden arms

NEW YORK, MYSELF AND ONE OTHER

1

Needs no I or You
to hide us from itself, being largely sediment;
cliffs of anonymity and a few
exceptional peaks honestly lacking distinction.
Mountains are like this, huge and not huge
outweighing our need to implicate
our passionate loquaciousness. Lorca, go home !
Walt, stop flogging yourself
with that corny ceremony of calling !

2

Why can't you speak ? (you know how I fear soliloquy)
Why should we have to move for entente ?
Taxi drivers are taxi drivers, they take you places, they . . .
The woman in the No. 5 bus who cries, "I must have a ride
in that Zeppelin !" What should I do —
trail her like Breton, find out that madness exists ?
The poets will meet on Wednesdays, Doomsdays, Thursday at 3 P.M.
[(the ballroom),
in Corso, in Ginsberg, in academic supermarkets, there, and there, in
underground committees, and in the most unessential lacunae; clocks,
[aborted beatitudes !

How did I know that those were negresses from Martinique ?
Because of scale in their gestures, their musical intelligence.
How did I know that Puerto Ricans actually exist in the city ?
I felt the dying of the magisterial — of tropical ideals.
How did I know that Harlem was Harlem ?
I saw that the greensward was gone, that nothing would grow in its
[place.
Why did I think *Eilshemius belongs to the past ?*
Because the sky would preclude the gentle spoof of his dreaming.
How did I sense the fulfillment of women as women ?
Because I felt their slack perversely, I was free to touch their
[magnificent clothes.

3

We've seen so much today
and yet so little impresses you (only the cry from the heart, your
                              [tragic corner of complaint).
Don't you feel the city clapping back beneath your steps,
can't you invent its cilia or its yeasty embededness ?
Isn't the name of a street indicative of something ?
A Hundred and Tenth (I'll say it for you)
how disciplined it sounds, how cold but how slyly secretly involved —
                              [rings with rings.
A hundred and nine, a hundred and eight . . .
domes and corrugation, a feeling of brass.

Should we go forward, back
                    (I'm waiting)
should there be cities, poems, persuasions, artichokes of words ?

IF SOMEONE WERE TO ASK ME

If someone were to ask me if this is the greatest age,
the sickest the most cleaned up intense the most immense in the matter
[of choice,
the blackest in wavy vinyl, the deadliest shootabout
and by far the most remote . . . ?

like we can read about it
as we swallow the hills that grow our death.

VANCOUVER

Something must give
either my pride
(which was always a liability) . . .
Showers of black-edged rejections
tar and feather my head,
multiple postcards with folds
bombard me from the royal mail boxes.

O my past
why have I kept you rolled and fragrant
as a ceremonial carpet ?
BLOOD They must be patches of dye !
And here I've preserved this thing,
a crazy brother with the icon of his sex.

Monday : the streets treat me as a convalescent.
Tuesday : the glands of the universities threaten me with impotence.
Wednesday : Miss Universe.
Thursday : the Japanese arrive leather-suited, neater than truncheons.
Friday : blue-brained girls with delicate noses.
Saturday : free.
Sunday : the elders parade in their lizard skins.
        The Inlet tunes its blast of ancestral blue.

BONNIE PARKER

as women killers are scarce even in the badlands of America
you were sure to be discovered dusted off for art respectability
in those modest Southern cabins with shattering glass in place of screens
made to shoot diamonds instead of death

of course the myth is more important the myth which started
with that terrible ambush that split you from the reflex of action
so beautiful in the context of U.S.A. so necessary to your end

from the movie ceremony we learn your age as
pearly fedora as upright sedan as dustbowl Okie camp
as Paris prostitute beret as Texas No-Man's intersection as
all suggestive rumbleseatopening joke as unpredictable service
                                    [spacestation ambiance
as lunchcounter Hemingway opening gambit and menace

Bonnie you were the kite of an age its unrepentent flyer
its country silences rivers melting into India
its vehicle junkyards its roadside endless stubble first in all the world
we must learn from you celebrate your violent acts
as they were our acts as well

we must believe
that you were stolen with your car
that the man who stole you was Barrow
that you were waiting and you were waitress (where)
that Barrow was beautiful
his smile was lucky
he showed you a gun

we must believe
that he was helpless
that he covered you with blood (other men's impotence)
that he sulked that he really wanted his share
that you grew lovely
that you lay down twice
that you shopped together innocently dressed

it's not that I think you knew but Clyde was IT Clyde was EVIL
the perfect glaze of sun was intentional that day
the porch door's squeak was holy talk its closing clack a binding
                                        [punctuation

when he asked you THE QUESTION what could you possibly feel but
                                        [YES
his eyes were the articulation of that feeling
his suit the sharpened banner of your loveless world

America chose you and that's why they call you back
the Eagle stuffed with male virginity has pecked at your cheek

Bonnie the killer
Bonnie who loved her mother
Bonnie the lover
Bonnie the skinny and mean
Bonnie the maiden the murderer
Bonnie the serf the waif
of
America's
RADICAL FREEDOM

SALUTE FOR JERRY RODOLITZ

A spiel of grace, an early sunprick for the imagined river;
so it begins as it begins for all the others; long-drawn sound of traffic,
milk bomb at the door, woman coughing uphaa uphaa uphaa.

Barring the way the moss-red brick of Care, grocery window through
which you silently crash swimming into the blood, morning hallucination
at which I have stared dumbfounded by its opacity.

Once you started to read the "sickness" disappeared. Light from the
[floor
became attentive. The bed stopped ingesting you through its labial
[tissues.
In fish-bright plane the courier sang. Rimbaud, Artaud, assembled at
[poem's weightless plunge.
The poem slowly withdrawn as if the Underground, your Love, had
[threatened a burning.

Perhaps I exaggerate, perhaps I was thrown at finding so unexpectedly,
[so perfectly
a brother so terribly open like a wound. The courier, your pimp-dead
[girl,
lost in physical blue her half-breasts plastered noons, her mouth of
[lights unyielding
like a thousand bloodied trilliums.

Jerry Rodolitz with sickness-spaniel hair, six containers of pills by
[unmade bed,
I want your recipe for incense, your Ginsberg-goddess landed,
I want your twenty-seven years in which you are dying live and
[unchanging.

ALEXA

I saw your blood today
and it was inky viridian
and as still as emeralds

white and thin
your face is like a pic-nic plate
never finally set
and constantly blowing away

the head of a troll
in a far too perfect snowscape
humour levelled over a leather mitt
is it you or my craziest self

I'm trying to cap
your exceptional lyrical emptiness
I haven't a chance Alexa

when you're broken by sex
to some foreign dignity
there'll always be this poem

PHOTOGRAPH OF CAMUS AND HIS CHILDREN
IN THE COUNTRYSIDE NEAR PARIS

all three are touching the grass
THE PASTORAL OF EUROPE
already the modes have changed
and we can smile at such period informality
poignant features of the Bourgeois scene
the black-bagged daughter physically out of focus
an eagerness that flows
from expectation

the twins on either side
he forms the centre of a flattened triangle
    all are touching the grass
the mystical totem of Freedom's Man
the seated Camus looks inward at the action
public image restrained but implied
private anguish tensed in its executor

onto the fingertips of his left hand
the boy
drops through a frame of arrested motion
spare and Mediterranean even his shirt
has been ironed by Europe's Art
the rough-drawn ball of his head
a continental trademark

everything touches the grass
the knapsack off to the rear
    (if that's what it is)
a sweater definite and black

the index finger of the girl
her still too clumsy knees
the fingertips the sandals of the boy
Camus' supporting hand
the base line
of a tri-
angle

ANNA AKHMATOVA

with nothing to add
your face became its worst imaginings
in the eyes
of the guildmembers
you had finally come to heel

the light compression of your lips
was torn by the
white breath of the crowd
a tyrant hid in the curtains
as you rhymed the famous evenings
auctioned
under the sill

love as part of the sea
(the sea was your imagined frontier)
as part of a green futility
flecked with blood
no wonder
they labelled you patriot

did poetry have to exist
your pages which fluttered and settled
the most remorseless word
your hopeless walks
the blackest of them all

I shouldn't ask

I read your poems
hurried to settle your claims
like a poor broker
I can tell by this picture
that you are
Stalin's murderess
Stalin's sister

ON THE DEATH OF CHE GUEVARA

his grave was dug
as his body huge as a flyer
lay on its arm

with death grows adoration
night helps
enormous hoops of smoke
the white man's poster resting on the eyes
of tired schoolgirls

as proof he'd lived his wife looks chic
(parenthood is not the pact of solidarity)
the children special and pathetic
Castro grave
mounting the monstrous texts
each citizen a word
each word the most phenomenal

here he rests thin as a skate
here he germinates above the crowd
beard unkempt or nubile (either has its value)
beret straight befitting an earnest heritor of Spain

Che
the smouldering priest of Marxtown
the hero rushed to production
in liquid Havana

AMERICAN DREAM POEM

who did it I wonder
who does it
not the two kids playing so purely with handcuffs
or the plump done buddhas dozing in the subway
or the morbid nurse discoursing on her patient's sores ...

although its windows are shining clean
nothing lives in the apartment house called ROSE ANNA
but here comes a moral lift a promising clue   I've noticed
a vast and perfectly distinguished place which might be
a hospital or a university or a publishing house ...

they who gave us the subway
gave to us the sweet black humour of the express
and a hundred blocks of peace   they gave us the underground stations
where people wait like haunted game

september is a palpable shock with its green skies
and its rivers running with blackish spotlights
with three red clouds over Jersey
and a deer I once saw bolting over the thruway
it's time for the binding of trees and for neon safety vests
it's time to drain the water round the beautiful dinosauric Moore
at Lincoln Centre

who does it
who
the ancient waitress shovelling dirty plates into the discard
the flower baby pale as a suppository
the hippies caught like children in the fumbled stare of the underground
                                                            [cinéaste

the museum guard in his bespectacled death mask
the cop in his fencing suit of murdered blue

ISOBEL ETC. REMEMBERED

Snow when it fell. I cooked sausages,
lay about troubled with too much life.
"You come too quick," says Isobel, switching priorities
sweeping then like Cinderella.

I was an astrologue, typical creep,
my stations of the muse above reproach —
Botticelli, *I had only to wish* LA PRIMAVERA.
The waitress in plaster blue,
I should have murdered the bitch
torn at her schizo breasts.

To wait if anyone could, watch and read
of SEX and beatings, sunset orgies every night.
O my captive cities, my placid son et lumière,
my sunlit retreats, my perfect constancies.

"Goin to the wrastlin." Isobel, I swore,
I'll cook your quiff, haunt you with cultured voyeurs,
cause you to fuck with your brother. She phones again.
"It's me." It's who ? "It's me," she yells, "Isobel, you cocksucker !"

AFTER READING SOME POEMS BY RED LANE

hexed by the crush of mountains
(deprived might be the better word)
the Pacific glamourized out of his view
a part of literature perhaps
which is part of the past
a complex taboo
space a bath of sunlight
for the dead brains he encountered
day after day
in farm trucks
drawing abreast of his freedom
in pinched Canadian towns
eating the Lord's own food
the drunks accosting him
that he accosts
girls their innocent giving
teasing an impotent rage
in doors which opened for him
doors which shut
the shrapnel of marginal kindness
trash like a
thousand fences in his way
and over these PRETENSION

MY LOVE WAS NEVER THE TIME

my love was never THE TIME
my love grew longer by the hour   no one
loves like this
not even the land not even that autumn of postcards
which had me on the ropes
for twenty years

it's like the Siberian gardener
tending his shelf of flowers
why not crystals   why not frozentanks of snow

people are living their lives (this is fact)
voices are urging defections   art and instruments
are aired by hand
with measurable care

I have to be serious
try to be heard
I could have missed my birth

BONNARD

Bonnard I salute you
when did you die

they say the young
people hate you because you
painted so religiously
left them your face
in the bathroom mirror
suicide place

I read how a wife
appeared out of nowhere
came to live in your
humble tub   festered in colour
pressed in a kind of
early thermography

joy was near
fruit stood ready to
disappear as did plaster
and leaf   the first fast cars
burned landscape as tornado
the dentist stood
by his gleaming chair

and radio came
spoke through its mandolin hole
and some old shaky plane
flew buzzing from
the last pages of your paint rag

LIGHT lights . . .

Light is a concept caught between its mythologies,
and meanwhile like shine of the blackest vinyl
we're soft on a second choice
of daylight, people-incandescence, ultimate contrasts, lights etcetera.

If I think of lights I think of an Edison older than Moses, a mural
Marx in Rochester or Ohio or wherever, a patriarch who'd overcome
                                                    [the worst —
THREE LONG MONTHS OF FORMAL EDUCATION.

I think of Talbot and Daguerre, of my great-great-grandmother before
                                                    [cosmetics,
before expressions; the beginning of Celluloid Time, brittle as
                                                    [fingernails,
freckled in crystals.

Lux, lumen, fohss, luce, licht, light . . . the absolutes before the absolute,
Before the advent of photons, Mazda, the phoney mantle of man —
a reckless promise of Light which has given us our GREATEST
                                                    [HANGUP
our most critical discolouration . . .

and the earliest of peep shows, an easier eye of the needle
a gift of heavenly neon laced in our native black;
the tender skin of the movies (close-up of kinetoscope)
the human weather of its blowups, its highways of graffitti, its blooming
and protracted forgeries.

114

As a poet
I pad the poets'
list of contributions : from
a muscled D'Annunzio,
his metals in
the Mediterranean sun;
the subway ride with
Crane, crashing forward into
the coloured eyes —
a first attempt
at psychedelia.

To quote myself, "the world is shiny, black, and clean, and faintly
[luminous;
active or serene the way a wheel spins backwards in the stroboscope."

An age of light, if we can make it as IT IS,
enter this fabulous word.

met two hippie priests on the road   offered them place
    I in my car   they on foot
mouton hats sexless beards   overcoats of the after-war
    they sublime   I intent on the laws of driving
                         so where do you live
I inquisitive   they content   the sea immense like
  blue myopia itself   the sun conducting its burning
  off in the deafness of space
                  the Island they say   the Island of course
then Boaz the forest primaeval   potlatch the morals of plenty
                     SPEND TILL IT HURTS
  they informative   I like a plant in the rain
                    they at peace
    unfolding the faith   the poem of their day

GENTLENESS

gentleness is one thing
few can afford
in your little apartment
I
was glad for the electric heater

you argued too long about money
but not with me
you poked your head in the door and said
I argue too long about money

I loved your picture then
even the frozen chair
I waited and thawed
inside our pact
of
gentleness

FOUR PART POEM

the Ace unpacked   the mountain mugged and stripped out of earshot

the leader's mission clears a final obstacle   once seen the lake goes
                                         [unmolested

the censored page explodes   the neatly folded blanket awaits the
                                         [prisoner's return

the Plan achieves projection B   only the zeros escape

COLLAGE POEM

sky — the incandescent weed of Mexico

love revolves the bandstand with its windlass of white exertions

his honour jingles coins

BANG   gives an air of easter skeletons
bang the rabbit   bang the pipe   bang the duck

the memoire is signed by the memoire

a fatal rip in the past   a feature rip in the present

bus as mightyass with figures recessed   as Coyocan

THE MOVIE DIRECTOR

a broken watch he broods a sprocket in the hangars of his coded gesture

immobilized his fingers pick the angles of the sofas of a thousand
[international hotel suites

he feels the way an owl flops into twilight   an aristocrat approaching
[the palace breakfast

inside the cabaret of feathers his muses climb like twisted foil

his agents sign the curtains of the ripest excavations

he phones to meet his childhood in an aged dog meandering on the
[pavement of an early morning

his schedule overlaps the open rhythms of the starlet's nose the puppet
[theatre of her hair

a cousin pricks the endless script or shuffles cards on which the legend
ACCIDENT appears in broken lights or FLOOD a one dimensional

his meta-hero scrofulous and tall confronts the trucks of progress with
[a roadblock of cellos

his credits peck the shovels of the workers' eyes

SYLVIA

your eyes which are the almond seeds of my desire

your hair which in spite of its island calm is the lava flow of my
                                        [absentee homeland

your mouth with its final and palpable P

your knees which instruct me in love's occult simplicity

your breasts with their fists of welcome their scale of peppermint flesh

your half-heard movements like the stiff collation of forests

your smile which cuts me off which opens Asia to the slaves

your image and your non-image   your honest and dishonest scents

your orphaned intelligence pausing in fright in the aisle of the Tax-Free
                                        [Supermarket

your painter's eye whose basic industry lightens the cupboards of missing
                                        [millionaires

your colours resealed in the menstrual flow of woman's blinded editorial

IF THEY KNEW HOW I THOUGHT

if they knew how I thought
they'd be trailing me and
shooting at the dark

if they knew how I felt
they'd swallow their children heads and all
as a safeguard

if they knew who I was
they'd say a mass for the
International Trade Union of the Dead

if they knew who I wanted to be
they'd double the lost blue wing
of Happiness Freeway

BETTY AND MARTIN'S LOFT

I would never imagine this —
a loft in the beard of the night
angles like iron primadonnas
and an eiderdown   art is un-manned
by such honest indulgence

I'm feeling strangely off balance
sickness is close like a country composed
of the strictest reds
     can't say why I'm so unsure

books and the clear-scoured woods
I'd like to aggress on these objects
that pass from love to love
close to the flesh
secretly
under the skirts
of flaming revolutions

they are a sickness too

TO ATHENS WITH LOVE

it was almost too beautiful to remember
rounding the corner of civilization the streets turned white and
the balconies ended
I was one of the living
and I hadn't sold any secrets to the U.S.A.

everyone dressed in black
cafes of exiled men stripped to their inalienable rights
post offices with postage stamps for wickets   empty directions
which led to a little-known suburb of Paris
gaiety fought against the Spartans and the light and the stillness
which had never retreated at Thermopylae

the Palace played waltzes for empty rooms
a crowded oasis dropped passcards for a night in the temple of Hygeia
I wasn't alone   the micro-centre had moved its approval
nor was I stalked by revenge
I wasn't seen as one of the loved

at breakfast (as sunlight lay on its litter)
I learned how the wine-black sea had broken its vase
lunchtime tourists were burning their guides
instead of their bleached imaginations
in place of supper the wolves of poverty
sank their teeth in the hills
and just as I reached for my light
the public scene aborted

what was my name
had my Greek been misinterpreted
did I like this city
was Lenin between my legs when I entered its limits

to catch my boat
I took the electric train
although the Piraeus suggested a wooden chute
or a walk in time to the guilt free rhythms of language

FOR THE SECOND TIME

for the second time
I ask the land for signs
put on your lost branched head-dress I explain
unscramble the veins of your bulging granite

how elegant we are
shining wealth
shining pools
and how exposed we look hunched
on our machines like scarecrows in
The Book of Simple Terrors

it may be irrational to note
that already some mountain peaks have set
(while fortune slept)
while oceans were bathing our yellow eyes

the crash-pad in which minorities
mortgage their frozen hands
is zoned for the soldiers of CORRECTION
and for poets
of similar faith

ON THE DEATH OF ROBERT TAYLOR
WHOSE ACTUAL NAME APPEARS BELOW

another star extinguished   this time
Spangler Arlington Brugh
                    he was
a glory flower of America
awkward with his numbered face   stiff of pace
grave in place of passionate
                         the thunder-resonance
of virgin man
AMERICA   AMERICA
                    freedom breaks
as cowboys herd the evening currencies
STAR remakes
with all that's single and perplexing

I saw a great volcano   a masterminded hole
clouds of food an empress swollen from the seed
of each defeated forest O AMERICA
I mourn you through the taste of oracles
the vestibule of accidents
a fever in the last autonomous partition

STILLNESS

stillness has
become
INCOMMUNICABLE

just this morning
burning banks in Santa Barbara
loosely falling clubs
from every channel

the golfer bird
of Phoenix Arizona
is a
chill exception

an instant irrefrangible
the hunter with
his boot on the herd skull

an anthropologist
who should LOVE
FATE
sagely swapping
green bananas

CHARLES OLSON AS THE OTHER

Letter Seven of the *Maximus Poems*
intervals and sounds withdrawn
like Eastern landscape
words of character provided like
moly and tansy

Marsden Hartley's hands
great
but tragic too
through specialization (dedication ?)
my poor land
with its inhuman treks
and hysterical silences
there to
begin

morning   morning has written the test
legs have frozen
unlocking the cash   washing
the cases clear with Windex   sweeping
angling vacuuming   music fixed
in the slot of waiting
like grass once was or distance simply
or even
dumb self interest

What has this to
do with me
what has
it
not

CLIMATE

this could be a poem
about cold or death or sensuality
or contradiction
the place is a delicatessen the
month November the principal actor
whatever he wanted to say said
"I'm sixty-seven and I'm going to die"
not die here I thought not in this poem
I was just beginning to handle flint and
the sidewalk   hibernation and window-glass
and what had I gone and said about winter...

    I remember Cape Cod — a beautiful couple
    who'd lived through war and art-fed mystical intelligence
    their car which always stood in attendance
    was a green torpedo-shaped Studebaker sedan
    (twenty thousand miles in fifteen years)
    when I sat on
    the beach with them
    it was Cannes in nineteen twenty-eight...
    "you know (the husband apologetically) we're seventy and
    we can't believe it"

"it's all been nothing pointless"
he continues madly   I look around at
the blood-puffed winter skins   overcoats hanging about
like discarded bladders   I bite in my smoked-meat sandwich
SEVEN LAYERS OF MEAT a hefty deposit in
The First Starvation Bank of America...
distract him I thought ask him
where the riot is
I really wanted to blurt that
he'd written a single marvellous poem   he had

I wanted to roll the event in a single word like "climate"

Delta Canada titles:

Collected Poetry, Louis Dudek

Selected Poems : 1920-1970, R.G. Everson

Les Eaux Remiroitées, Henry Miller
    (trad. par Gérald Robitaille)
    French-English edition

Printed
by
Les Ateliers
Jacques Gaudet Ltée,
St-Hyacinthe,
Canada